Illuminating Strength and Hope

Sandra W. Smith

Illuminating Strength and Hope
Copyright @2024

Illustrations and Formatting @2024

All rights reserved.
This book or any portion thereof may not be reproduced or used in any manner whatsoever without written permission.

Printed in the United States of America by SCSxpressions

ISBN : 979-8-9893090-5-4

Library of Congress Number
2024917056

DEDICATED

To all those who seek wisdom and hope in the blessings all around us. May these inspiring words, written with you in mind, guide your daily journey.

With much gratitude, may the love of the Almighty light your way. This book is dedicated to you.

Inspiring words have a way of easing pain, renewing the spirit, and providing life-giving hope. Throughout my life, I have clung to powerful statements, uplifting quotes, and endearing words that propelled me forward and offered immense encouragement. I hope you find inspiration in my book of quotes, enriched with meaningful insights to empower and fill you with joy.

Sandra Smith

WHY I WROTE THIS SPECIAL BOOK

As someone who deeply loves God, cherishes nature, and the serenity they bring, I am passionate about sharing life-giving inspiration through enriching words of quotes. My hope is that these quotes will offer you strength, calm, and the fortitude to pursue your goals and embrace life's challenges and opportunities while interacting with our Creator through nature.

This book is an invitation to connect, to give yourself permission to simply be, to release taxing thoughts seeking to consume, and to be at peace. Each quote is accompanied by thoughtful analysis designed to help you find refreshment and inspiration as you take intentional moments of stillness. Life is a journey full of new beginnings, and as you read, experience the beauty and vitality of these words.

I wrote this book with you in mind, aiming to offer you peace and encouragement. My hope is that you will take the time to read, reflect, meditate, and even share these quotes with others. May the blessings around you be yours to behold, and always remember that you are enough.

THE GOALS FOR THE BOOK:

- To help you feel refreshed and encouraged as you explore nature.

- To enable you to experience the presence of the Creator through your interactions with nature.

- To inspire you to read, reflect, and let the essence of these words touch your heart.

- To encourage you to meditate, relax, and find peace.

- To motivate you to grow, reach out, and recognize your own awesomeness.

Enjoy this gift of inspiration, and may it infuse your life with renewed purpose and joy.

HOW TO USE THE BOOK

Read a quote a day, reread and then use it in some way.

Memorize at least one quote a week or bi-monthly.

Start writing your favorite quotes on post it-notes or index cards.

Meditate on your favorite quote.

Note your favorite quote, write it down and see how it has affected you in some way.

Share your favorite quote with someone.

Write down several encouraging quotes within a month and give others a copy.

Write your best quote on a notecard and put it in your favorite place.

Share aspects of the book with someone special.

Have a quote sharing and discussion lunch with a few friends.

Come up with your own idea of how to incorporate the power of enriching quotes.

Read, re-read and then read some more.

1

Nature's Wisdom Sunlight and Celestial Inspiration

Refreshing waterfalls of goodness generously nourish the habitat of my thirsty soul.

Through knowing God, we have all we need. His abundant love is a serene, quiet waterfall of upliftment.

*I relish
God's riveting artistry of
bountiful
love, pervasive all
around me.*

The love of God manifests through creation—the towering trees, the vast oceans, and precious smiles—fills me with gratitude.

Illustrious sunbeams of hope peek through expansive windows extending shimmering rays of steadfast endurance.

Hope guides and brightens the way providing strength and resolute determination.

Embrace this glorious day with outstretched hands ready to grasp all God has ordained to keep you close.

Welcome each day with a grateful heart actively seeking to receive blessings and guidance that have been divinely prepared for you.

Humbled by your rainbow of love, Lord, teach me to earnestly pray and align my will with yours.

God's immeasurable love, overflows with compassion and grace; I'm humbled to seek Him and live a gracious life.

*As I consciously sit spellbound by the tranquil ocean of love,
I overwhelmingly grasp God's abundant power.*

I'm awed by God's love for me, and I'm at peace in His magnificent presence. Everything will be just fine, for His power is my strength.

*God's omnipotent and
glorious creation
is a nurturing hand
of assurance and peace.*

God continuously guides and reassures us
throughout life's journey.

Fluffy clouds of discovery bestow resounding awareness and indispensable encouragement throughout life's journey.

Being intentional, making discoveries, and reflecting on life provides enlightened growth and strength.

You are compassionately adorned and graced with God's unconditional gift of love.

It's wonderful knowing we don't have to do anything to earn God's kindness and love; our abundant lives are freely given. We are loved unconditionally.

God's miraculous, illustrated creation magnifies His unveiling power and magnificent glory.

I'm awed by God's immeasurable power and glorious splendor.

A tranquil glimpse of heaven's illuminating light reflects designed purpose and triumphant victory.

Learning to be still intentionally and at peace renders not only calm, but the clarity of designed purpose.

The prevalence of God's majestic creation greets me with audacious grandeur and promise, propelling me to rejoice in expectation.

As I look around and embrace the beautiful wonders of God, His magnificent creation evokes hope and confidence, bringing joy and inspiration.

God's enchanting workmanship of splendor profoundly eases my fears, lovingly guiding me with murals of prevailing faith.

Be strengthened and inspired through divine guidance as you observe God's majestic creation.

*The exalted canvas of
celestial beauty
birth harmonious melodies
of gleaming hope.*

The radiance of heaven brings captivating hope and lasting peace.

Luminous stars glisten ever so bright, releasing altitudes of exuberant joy beyond measure.

Stay focused on the illuminating stars, for they bring immense joy.

When reflecting on the nature quotes you read, choose the one that resonates with you the most, and write why.

When reflecting on the nature quotes you read, choose the one that resonates with you the most and write why.

2

Serene Oceans, Rivers, and Streams of Time

Streams, oceans, and rivers are calming allurements for the soul, soothing our anxieties and bringing immense serenity and resolve.

The beckoning and harmonious shores of acceptance refresh my receptive heart ushering consoling embrace and respect.

Accepting ourselves and others ushers in the welcoming and revitalizing arms of comfort and respect, creating a place where we all belong.

Tranquil oceans of respect usher fragrant blessings of love.

Our respectful relationship blossoms with love.

Inspiring flowing rivers cascade consoling and peaceful hugs of cheer.

Seeing a beautiful, serene body of water soothes and uplifts, bringing reassuring waves of motivation and inspiration.

Humbly basking in an ocean of unconditional love is a fountain of liberating joy.

Absolute love is an infinite reservoir of immense joy.

The refreshing whispers of the sea emit soothing pleasantries of solace, conferring triumphant strength and assurance.

Calming whispers of the sea are strengthening gifts.

Breathtaking streams of abundance affectionately salute the enthralling and prominent Lordship of our Mighty God.

I am deeply grateful for the abundant blessings and goodness bestowed upon me from above.

What a wonder to behold the mesmerizing and beautiful orchestra of picturesque rivers.

Captivating rivers of life are a harmonious symphony of blessings.

Hear the gentle and consoling voice of yesterday's shores conveying goodness and a purposeful beginning.

Echoes of the past bring freeing and reassuring experiences of wisdom and new beginnings.

God's peaceful presence affectionately eases my climatic fears with nurturing waves of prevalent faith.

The peaceful and faithful presence of God relieves my anxieties and concerns.

*Oceans of love cry out,
ushering gentle waves
of soothing affection and
quiet reassurance.*

The profound depth of love is soothing tranquility.

The compelling streams of affirming trust manifest victorious rivers of fortitude and courage.

Consistent assurance fosters confidence and determination.

The beautiful, tranquil reservoir of wisdom, birth enlightening seas of confidence.

Peaceful and insightful understanding illuminates self-assurance.

Refreshing rivers of consolation bestow overflowing streams of tranquility.

Comforting solace brings deep calm and stillness.

The melodious waves of sweet peace dispense anchored contentment and expansive solitude.

Peaceful moments of contentment embrace alone time.

The rolling tides of life emit peaceful waves of immense beauty.

There is beauty in challenges and change, garnished in sweet peace.

When reflecting on the nature quotes you just read, choose the one that resonates with you the most and write why.

When reflecting on the nature quotes you just read, choose the one that resonates with you the most and write why.

3

Blossoms of Renewal

Beautiful, refreshing flowers are reservoirs of rejuvenation and liberating freshness.

Enchanting flowers of copious strength surrender refreshing petals of hope and boundless cheer.

The resilience of a beautiful flower inspires both confidence and joy.

Cherishing your incredulous splendor accelerates flourishing heights of immense gratitude.

Your captivating demeanor is deeply appreciated and valued.

Your vibrant compassion rejuvenates my aching heart, catapulting promise and blossoming renewal.

Kindness and compassion revitalize and spurs desire and hope.

God's peaceful presence of exuberant color is a garden of insurmountable and transcending love.

Like a flourishing, vibrant garden, the immeasurable love of God surpasses everything.

Lord, your majestic canopy of countless compassion and blessings confers renewed hope and comfort.

I revere you Lord, for your unspeakable graciousness and peace.

The alluring beauty of life's flourishing flowers usher faith and appreciation, affirming I'm resilient and complete.

The blooming of enchanting flowers rejuvenate me with gratitude, fostering resilience and strength.

Your delicate and exquisite petals of strength promenade peaceful energies of purpose and stillness.

Your purposeful strength radiates an inner calm and peace.

I'm forever inspired by awakening flowers of radiant delight and benevolent affection.

Glorious flowers bring boundless inspiration.

*As you gracefully extend
your receptive arms,
I instantaneously feel the
garnishing embrace
of victory.*

Acceptance is a triumphant success.

Your debonair presence of beauty fosters cascading colors of confidence and humility.

Your engaging presence exudes courage and reassurance.

Life's promenading whispers of hope serenade tulips of contentment and fragrant aspirations.

Life's journey whispers gently, inspiring beauty and hope.

The beautiful blossoming flowers of kindness magnify fragrant aromas of self-worth, affirming I am enough.

Your flourishing warmth radiates positivity.

Strengthening challenges nourish my soul with bountiful bouquets of promise.

Obstacles bring enriching assurance.

Keep soaring to destined heights swaddled in passionate faith and fortitude.

Faith and inner strength propel you forward.

Our treasured and unbreakable friendship is an unconditional ocean of harmony.

Our cherished relationship is a serene sea of support.

Life's mountainous valleys of strength produce stabilizing forces of comfort.

Life's challenges become sources of stability and comfort, making us stronger.

Keep growing and prevailing through life's uncertainties with fearless faith and fervent prayer.

Despite life's adversities, remain steadfast in prayer and faith.

Ascend to God-ordained heights anchored in joyous rivers of steadfastness.

God's purpose flourishes in volumes of dedication and joy.

*I'm enamored with God's
prevailing presence
and indescribable goodness.*

Revere almighty God.

*The gratifying petals
of yesterday
are riveting rainbows
of greatness.*

The joys of yesterday are enriching.

Mountains of fervent prayer are enchanting reservoirs of blessings.

Earnest prayers are stored blessings.

Flowing waters of strengthening tides are vibrant friendships of love.

Devoted relationships are unbreakable bonds.

Melodious friendships of trust are a treasure chest of priceless jewels.

Our cherished relationship is irreplaceable.

Revere the glorious and powerful tapestry of the Master's touch.

Creation is magnificently esteemed.

Beckoning shores of acceptance, refresh my receptive heart with loving care.

A welcoming embrace is truly invigorating.

Beautiful petals of kindness administer undeniable blessing of grace.

Warm-heartedness bestows gracious blessings.

When reflecting on the nature quotes you just read, choose the one that resonates with you the most and write why.

When reflecting on the nature quotes you just read, choose the one that resonates with you the most and write why.

My favorite quotes in the book are

Find deep inspiration to believe, persevere, and gain strength as you observe and interact with nature. Life is filled with mesmerizing rivers and fragrant flowers, so keep seeing the beauty in all things. There are numerous blessings to behold all around you.

Inspiring Hope

I sincerely hope this heartfelt collection of quotes, life-affirming messages, and profound insights has filled you with joy and hope, uplifted your spirit, and inspired you.

Milton Keynes UK
Ingram Content Group UK Ltd.
UKHW050824211124
3020UKWH00003B/4